Keepers of the Flame

Devotions For Military Spouses

KEEPERS of the FLAME

DEVOTIONS FOR MILITARY SPOUSES

Judy P. Davis

Belleville, Ontario, Canada

Keepers of the Flame
Copyright © 2004, Judy P. Davis

National Library of Canada Cataloguing in Publication

Davis, Judy P., 1943-
Keepers of the flame : devotions for military spouses / Judy P. Davis.
ISBN 1-55306-701-0

    1. Families of military personnel--Prayer books and devotions--English. I. Title.

BV4588.D38 2004   248.8'6   C2004-900033-0

For more information or
to order additional copies, please contact:

Judy Davis
judys12@juno.com
www.flwriters.org/judydavis.htm

Guardian Books is an imprint of Essence Publishing, a Christian Book Publisher dedicated to furthering the work of Christ through the written word. For more information, contact:
20 Hanna Court, Belleville, Ontario, Canada K8P 5J2
Phone: 1-800-238-6376 • Fax: (613) 962-3055
E-mail: publishing@essencegroup.com
Internet: www.essencegroup.com

This book is dedicated to all those individuals
who have faithfully served our country,

To my husband of thirty-seven years,
Colin Davis,
who served in Vietnam,

And to those left behind to carry on.

May God bless you,
and
may God continue to bless America.

"If my people, who are called by my name, will humble themselves and pray and seek my face and turn from their wicked ways, then I will hear from heaven and will forgive their sin and will heal their land" (2 Chronicles 7:14).

A Personal Prayer for Salvation

Father,

Thank you for all you do for us each day. I come as a little child to sit at your feet as we together face the trials and tribulations that continue to touch our lives. During times of conflict may we always turn to you for it is your hand that delivers us from evil.

I admit I have sinned and fall short of your glory. "For all have sinned and fall short of the glory of God" (Romans 3:23).

I believe in Jesus Christ, the Son of God, who died to set me free. "For God so loved the world that he gave his one and only Son, that who ever believes in him shall not perish but have eternal life" (John 3:16).

Help me today as I confess my sin to you. "If we confess our sins, he is faithful and just and will forgive us our sins and purify us from all unrighteousness" (1 John 1:9).

Amen

Submit yourselves for the Lord's sake to every authority instituted among men: whether to the king, as the supreme authority, or to governors, who are sent by him to punish those who do wrong and to commend those who do right (1 Peter 2:13-14).

Table of Contents

Introduction

*A*s I write the pages of this devotional book, it's my desire to reach out and touch not only the men and women who sacrificed their lives for our country but the many military spouses who were left behind to carry on. Colin, my husband of thirty-seven years, served his country for over forty years in the Air Force. We were only married three months when he left for Vietnam. One of my greatest memories while my husband was overseas was the day the newspaper carried this letter:

> Dear Editor:
> I am serving in Vietnam at this time, returning to the United States in December. I would like for you to print the following: To my wife, Judy Davis, on our anniversary;

Happy First Anniversary, Darling. Thinking of you on this special day. Our first happy year and looking forward to many more just as happy.

Over here a few things are very hard to get a hold of. I can't find an anniversary card. I married a girl from Warner Robins, Georgia, and she is still living there.

That was in 1966. I knew when I married him that he would have to leave, but nothing prepared me for the day he left. "Please God, let him return," was my prayer.

His letters came regularly; we both wrote each day. There were many beautiful memories like going to see him in Hawaii. I met him there on R and R (Rest and Recuperation). Also, I remember the day the florist delivered beautiful roses and a corsage on my birthday. Then there was the day the telephone call came from him. I couldn't believe I was talking to him and him so far away; yet it was as if he were in the same room. He had to stand in line for hours waiting to call me.

There were also the painful memories. Every time I watched the news I would see fighting and horrible scenes. I'll never forget the day I heard Colin's base had been hit. As I watched the news I thought, "Will he return? How much will he be affected by this war?" I prayed, "Please, God, let us be together on our next anniversary."

I'll never forget the day he returned. I baked his favorite chocolate cake. I had my hair styled. Everything had to be perfect. Going to the airport I kept thinking, "Will he be the same?"

As he got off the airplane, I ran to meet him with tears in my eyes and joy in my heart. He looked different;

he was thinner and seemed quieter. Had he changed? Yes, he could never be the same person he was when he left. He had seen another way of life. He had been on a journey afflicted with sorrow.

The memories will always be in my heart. We have now been married for thirty-seven years and have seen many changes since the Vietnam era. We have three married children and five grandchildren. The most important change is how we have grown together spiritually.

I continue to thank God for bringing Colin safely home and for the healing in his life from what he left behind. I thank God for each day He has given to us.

Farewell

Peace in the Midst of the Storm

"Peace I leave with you; my peace I give you; I do not give to you as the world gives. Do not let your hearts be troubled and do not be afraid."

—John 14:27

*J*esus was comforting his disciples during times of trial and unrest just as he comforts us today. A young wife discovers she is expecting again, their third child. Her husband walks in the door and calmly says: "I received orders for overseas and will leave this week; but can not tell you where I'll be as it is classified information." These are the kinds of traumas that are facing our military families. How do they cope? They pray and seek God for divine guidance.

Talking with my friend, she tells me she is 100 per cent comfortable with his going to war. She feels at peace. "This is what we signed up for... I feel proud that our family is serving our country. My husband recently re-enlisted in the Air Force in November and is ready to move forward in whatever direction God is leading. Our children wear badges with their dad's picture. We'll e-mail every day."

Linda's family lives in another state but plans to help when they can. Her main support is other military wives living on base who are facing the same struggles.

The base chapel serves a dinner each Wednesday evening. Linda plans on taking her children and talking with other wives in the same situation. They will fellowship, pray and move forward together as they endure the long days and months ahead waiting for their husbands to return from war.

How can we have the peace that Christ longs for us to have? We must search the Scriptures with all our heart and cling to them. And "peace, peace, wonderful peace," the words from a song we sing in our choir, will be restored to our lives as we trust in Him.

Life Goes On

*"Therefore do not worry about tomorrow;
for tomorrow will worry about itself. Each
day has enough trouble of its own."*

—*Matthew 6:34*

*L*ife becomes scarier for husbands and wives of military personnel sent to fight the war against Iraq. The spouses are waiting and hoping for the best, giving all the support they can from so far away. Having children makes the job of military spouses even tougher.

"We're very, very busy," Jane said as she wrestled with her son. "We don't worry. My husband told us not to worry. It's in the Lord's hands. It's just sad."

It's usually the wives that stay behind, however, Larry, twenty-nine, finds himself in an unusual situation. His wife shipped out last week, and he summed it up in two words, "It's weird."

Another spouse, Barbara, says she tries to reassure her husband that everything is all right at home. "He'll

Judy P. Davis

ask, 'How's everything?' You have to say, 'It's great.' I put on a front when he calls."

Their seven-year-old daughter is having a difficult time with her father gone. She doesn't know how to handle it and is stressed out. Barbara has found comfort in her faith and fellow church members. "I'm concentrating on doing a lot more praying than worrying," and she focuses on their four children. "If I'm okay, they are okay."

We can be anxious or calm—we make a choice each day. Choose today to walk in calmness, allowing Jesus Christ to lead the way.

On the Home Front

Finally brothers, whatever is true, whatever is noble, whatever is right,
whatever is pure, whatever is lovely, whatever is admirable—
if anything is excellent or praiseworthy—
think about such thing.

—*Philippians 4:8*

*P*aul was writing to the Christians at Philippi, explaining to them the importance of keeping their hearts and thoughts right before God. Sometimes it is difficult to keep our thoughts on those things that are good and pure, but knowing this is what will help us during times of conflict is the key to overcoming during this time of stress.

"News of the war changed things quickly," said Ann. "It's really affecting our two teenagers. It's hit home that Dad is gone. We are trying to stay upbeat. The three of us girls have been rather glued to the TV. The war is here and now, and it's very real to us. Things are particularly tough for Kristy, who is scheduled to graduate from high school in May and would love for her dad to be there."

"He's been the person to push me. He's encouraged me," said Kristy.

"We all are trying to keep a positive attitude. Knowing Don is serving his country makes it easier for us to wait for him to come home. We are very proud of him."

As we face each new day, the right attitude with a pure heart will help us prevail during these long days and nights of conflict.

Sisters-in-War

*In addition to this, take up the shield of
faith, with which you can extinguish
all the flaming arrows of the evil one.*

—*Ephesians 6:16*

"You can't help but think about a chaplain and a colonel knocking on your door. I can just imagine myself answering that door. I'd be screaming," stated Chris. She and her sister-in-law, Dawn, are married to brothers who are overseas.

How do they handle this adversity? They have learned the family jobs their husbands did. Their husbands both took care of finances. "And you learn how to be a single parent real quick," said Dawn.

The children can be tiring but they keep their moms from going crazy worrying about the soldiers. Chris focuses on the little fellow in her life, the one who depends on her.

The women also garden, work out, and listen to music to cope with the stress. Although Dawn is not deeply devout, she has been looking up war and evil lately in the Bible that always sits on the coffee table.

Neither Chris nor Dawn let the present distress prevent them from preparing for their future. Both are enrolling in courses at the local college. They keep their spirits up, kidding around and laughing.

Dawn says, "I'm concerned about what our husbands will see and if they'll come home changed." But they too will find the wives who never left have changed, too. They have become more independent, stronger, and maybe a little more stubborn. All wars are not fought by the military. Some are waged at home, one day at a time.

Wedding Day Changed

Rejoice in the wife of your youth.

—*Proverbs 5:18*

*B*rides and bridegrooms are rushing to the altar afraid to wait until their beloved returns from war. Marriage is sacred and many choose to go ahead with their wedding plans.

Weddings are so special, Jesus even performed his first miracle at a wedding.

A big May wedding was planned but the couple said "I do" recently at the county courthouse. Cathy, the young bride, stated: "I don't want to miss the opportunity of marrying the love of my life." Her bridegroom, Joe, said he wanted to make sure she was provided for should the worst happen.

The couple said the best defense to the war in Iraq was a strong offense: marriage.

Because marriage is a lifetime commitment, the chaplain stated he counsels couples to wait, to ensure the decision is not based on emotions and the pressure of war but on careful thought and deliberation with sound advice.

Judy P. Davis

When her husband-to-be received orders to go, Cathy had only twenty-four hours to prepare for the wedding at the courthouse.

Coping With Uncertainty

No one serving as a soldier gets involved in civilian affairs—he wants to please his commanding officer.

—2 Timothy 2:4

Bonnie tries to make home life as normal as possible for their three children. She also leads a support group on the base. "I try to discourage spouses from watching too much news," she said. "A little [news] in the morning and some at night to get recaps is all you need."

Having children in the house is another reason she minimizes time spent watching the news. "Those of us with children old enough to understand the news have to be really careful of even having the news on in the background.

"The increased level of fighting has to happen and it absolutely scares me to death. But our soldiers are extremely well trained, know what they need to do and how to do it."

A soldier cannot focus on his or her mission if they are worried about their family back home.

"We encourage lots of activities in our group for our own sanity and that of our children," Bonnie said. "We get together as much as possible, even if there is laundry or errands to do. The bottom line is that we all try and watch out for each other and help each other. Just being in the company of others who have the same anxieties and stresses is a great comfort."

Eyes On the Conflict

On my bed I remember you; I think of you through the watches of the night.
Because you are my help, I sing in the shadow of your wings.

—Psalm 63:6-7

Candy slips away to the break room at work to pray, knowing God is watching over her during this time of strife. She watches TV for developments in Iraq that could affect her stepson stationed in Kuwait. "I always look to see if it's his unit on television," she said. Candy is on the clock during her TV breaks, but her bosses don't mind. They are among employers across the nation who say they have relaxed their rules in an effort to help workers with loved ones in the military. Company-sanctioned breaks to check television, radio and internet reports have become part of the workday in some places.

In Virginia, employees are allowed more liberal use of e-mail during work to keep in touch with relatives or friends in combat zones. "The bottom line is that if these men and women can leave their homes, jobs and families to protect our freedom, then the least we can do is to help family and friends stay in touch with them while they are away," Governor Mark Warner said.

Prayers and Support

Therefore, confess your sins to each other, and pray for each other....

—James 5:16

*J*oy, whose husband was deployed last month, said the support and prayers from the gals in her husband's office have been great. They call at least once a week to make sure everything is okay and that she doesn't need anything. What a blessing to have such caring co-workers.

A manager of a Wal-Mart store said he wouldn't stand in the way of his employees helping one another. They take breaks together and watch war news on one of the many televisions in the store.

Many companies are helping their employees by allowing them to take leave to console their families.

Moms-To-Be Face Added Burden

Hear my cry, O God; listen to my prayer. From the ends of earth I call to you. I call as my heart grows faint; lead me to the rock that is higher than I.

—*Psalm 61:1-2*

*O*nly through prayer and the comfort of God can these expectant mothers face this lonely time without their husbands.

Through letters and ultrasound pictures, nineteen-year-old Sharon tries the best she can to keep her husband updated on the progress of the twin boys she expects to deliver later this spring.

And while she tries to comfort him, she and countless other military wives must cope with the trials of pregnancy knowing that their husbands are thousands of miles away at war.

"I am scared," said Sharon, whose husband, Mitch, left for the Middle East in February. "I know that if he was here I still would be scared. But with him gone, I know it's going to be even more difficult."

Among the ninety-one American soldiers killed since the war with Iraq began last month, at least five died as expectant fathers.

A Good Name

A good name is more desirable than great riches; to be esteemed is better than silver or gold.

—*Proverbs 22:1*

Every time Hilda hears of a U.S. soldier's death, she can't help thinking it could be her husband, who is among the more than 17,000 soldiers of the 101st Airborne Division deployed in the Persian Gulf.

Expectant wives of deployed soldiers face everything from the fears of combat death to having to make important medical and financial decisions without their mate's immediate input.

And while the women watch the war play out on television, expectant fathers aren't there for prenatal doctor visits, shopping for baby gear or offering a quick massage for swollen feet and sore backs.

Women who give birth during the war know it's doubtful their husbands will be able to get home or to even know when they go into labor.

Hilda said she hopes to speak with her husband before her June due date because she wants to change the baby's planned name from Savanah Grace to Lana Ashton. "I've been joking that if I don't get to talk to him before then he'll just get a Red Cross message that says, 'Sorry, honey, I changed the name,'" she said.

Renew a Steadfast Spirit
Within Me

*Create in me a pure heart, O God, and
renew a steadfast spirit within me.*

—Psalm 51:10

anet feels that women living in the military
have no choice but to deal with their husbands
being gone for long stretches. Aside from
caring for their four-year-old daughter, Hattie,
Janet is expecting their second daughter in early May.
Her husband left for the Middle East in late February.

"I'm a pretty independent person. You have to be if
you're going to be married to someone in the military,"
Janet said. "Of course I'm emotional, but I have a four
year old so I have to be strong."

For support, many women turn to family, friends
and base support groups. Others rely on Operation
Special Delivery, which provides volunteers to help
pregnant military wives.

Janet's mother plans to move in with her daughter
within the next month. "The biggest thing I think is
trying to keep her spirits up, because he's not here."

"Mom and Dad can do so much, but they can't replace Jack."

God will Comfort Us During Times of Suffering

Who comforts us in all our troubles, so that we can comfort those in any trouble with the comfort we ourselves have received from God.

—2 Corinthians 1:4

Pat, national director of the nonprofit organization Operation Special Delivery, said volunteers have helped about 100 pregnant military wives nationwide since the September 11, 2001, terrorist attack.

"Within the last month, applications for their help have increased to about ten per week. The program offers women prenatal support and someone to be with them in the delivery room.

"The most important thing for any husband to do during labor is to be there and to touch her and hold her hand, but if that person is not there for those two crucial points then they're already starting out with a great loss," Pat stated.

Caring One for Another

"I know your deeds, that you are neither cold nor hot. I wish you were either one or the other!"

—*Revelation 3:15*

Jesus was speaking to the church at Laodicea. He was saying, "Do not be lukewarm; go and make disciples." Reading my newspaper, I read of a military wife receiving a hundred roses from her deployed husband. He wrote: "These roses are for my undying love I have for you and the promise of a more precious future together." My heart went out to her and others.

What can we do to help? Several churches in our area have started support groups to minister to these women. We have prayer, Bible study and fellowship and are available if needed.

Jesus is speaking to us today. We can live a life moving forward in Him—or stay in our own comfort zone.

In the Palm of His Hand

He who dwells in the shelter of the Most High will abide in the shadow of the almighty.

—Psalm 91:1

When Laura was asked what, if she could say anything to her husband, would she say, Laura replied, "Tad, I love you and miss you with all my heart. I support you in everything you are doing and know you will do a great job. I pray that the Lord would provide an endless well for you to draw courage, strength and wisdom from. We all pray for the protection of each of our American soldiers deployed, and I ask the Lord to hold each of you in the palm of his hand. Be strong."

"When Tad told me he was deploying, I was, of course, not surprised, given the country was preparing for war. I tried to be supportive, even though we had only been married nine days. While Tad was overseas, I knew he was feeling needy and vulnerable just as those of us who were left behind. I would write and let him know of my love and support daily. I also wanted to keep him involved in what was going on here in America."

A Mission of Love

"A new command I give you: Love one another. As I have loved you, so you must love one another."

—*John: 19 34*

"I believe in Jesus, and I don't think I was put down here to just serve lunches. He put me here to try to make a difference," said Grace, who serves flight lunches to the military.

"If I can make one person smile and go out the door looking happier than when they came in, I have done what my Father wanted me to do." She was referring to her heavenly Father and the ministry she believes he gave her—to love. She loves generously, and her reward is in seeing people happy. "People always tell me I have an unrealistic view of things, but I feel like you can love anybody," she said. "Kindness can't hurt me, and I'm so kind, how can you hurt me anyway? I'm going to care no matter what, it gives me so much peace."

When members of the service where Grace works depart for overseas, she shows up at the departure point at 4:00 a.m., three hours before her workday officially begins, to send everyone off with a hug. "I do it because I love them," she said. "It's kind of sad... you feel like one of your kids is leaving."

A Star in the Window

God set them in the expanse of the sky to give light on the earth.

—*Genesis 1:17*

A big salute to Faith Evangelical Lutheran Church, as this church honors all members who have been deployed, not only with prayers, love and gratitude for their willingness to sacrifice their comforts, but in a special way. A star has been placed in a window at the church to represent each deployed person.

The stars are illuminated twenty-four hours a day with an electric candle. On each star are the name, rank, and branch of service of one member. Additionally, all service members are on an honor roll on the wall in the sanctuary.

One member of the congregation had several of her family members deployed in Iraq. She stayed busy sending her loved ones little packages of different items that they could not buy overseas.

Homecoming

Homecoming Feast

"Observe the days as days of feasting and joy and giving presents of food to one another."

—*Esther 9:22*

Like most moms with a son overseas in the aftermath of the Iraqi war, Benji waits for that happy reunion when he returns to the States. "We're going to fix up a feast for him," Benji said. "We'll fix all his favorites—spicy collards, cheesecake and barbecue ribs."

She remembers the words she spoke to him when she gave him a parting hug. "We're going to pray for you. I love you and take care."

There's no word on when her son may come home. The original mission was estimated to take from six months to a year. "When the war first began, all I would do was watch TV from the time I woke up until I went to bed. I'd fall asleep watching the news, and when I woke up, it would still be on."

Benji decided to turn off the TV, pray more and try

not to worry. She also decided to focus on what she could do—like filling up a care package for him.

"I knew the war was coming, but you never think it will happen to you—that you'll have a child in a war. I respect what he's doing. I respect his decision. And I'm proud of him." Benji said if she could only relay one message to her son it would be: "I'm praying for you every day. We love you, and hurry home."

Reunion Joys

We who are still alive and are left will be caught up together with them in the clouds to meet the Lord in the air. And so we will be with the Lord forever.

—1 Thessalonians 4 17

A friend sent me the following about the USS Shiloh's return after ten months at sea. The returning service personnel were anxiously looking for familiar faces in the crowds. Emotions ran high with joy and excitement.

Eighteen men were meeting sons or daughters for the first time. Watching one sailor feeding his infant son was an emotional moment for everyone who shared in his joy.

At the same time, the return was bittersweet for those who had lost loved ones in the war dubbed "Iraqi Freedom." To underscore the irony of the homecoming, even as the USS Shiloh was docking, news reports were coming in that two more servicemen had been killed and seven wounded.

Reunions likewise are taking place at other bases

throughout the United States. Servicemen and women are making the long trip home from places they previously only knew about from world maps and history books. The joy of reunions is sweet.

The gathering of the people refers to that great reunion when Jesus Christ, the Messiah, returns. The wars in the Middle East are but the birth pangs of the second coming of Christ. As we continue to hear about our military men and women returning, let it remind us that one day soon our Lord will return... and unto him shall the gathering of the people be. I plan to be in this reunion. How about you?

Waiting for Daddy

"I will turn their mourning into gladness...."
—*Jeremiah 31:13*

A hot tarmac engulfed with the smell of jet exhaust is an unusual place for a twenty-month-old girl wearing a Sunday dress. But that's where Joanne was Monday morning. She was waiting for her daddy to come home.

Joanne and her mother Sue embraced Brian on the tarmac just a few yards from the plane that carried him home. It was Brian's first deployment and his first homecoming.

"I feel a lot of joy," said Sue. "I guess you could say it's rapture."

Her husband felt the same and said the first thing on his agenda was some quality time with Sue and Joann. Later, he would have some food. What type of food didn't matter, just "anything American."

USS *Lincoln* Returns to Home Port

Be happy, young man, while you are young, and let your heart give you joy in your youth.

—Ecclesiastes 11:9

After nearly ten months at sea, the USS Abraham Lincoln returned to its home port, greeted by thousands deliriously waving signs, blowing kisses and carrying red, white and blue balloons.

About 3,000 sailors were aboard the nuclear-powered aircraft carrier, which tied up to its home pier at Naval Station Everett.

"I think it's awesome," said a student, who was among the welcoming throng. "They went out for ten months to protect a lot of people, and now they get to come home."

The first to disembark were to be the ship's eighty-seven new dads, whose wives and babies were waiting at the front of the giddy crowd. Also at the head of the line were thirteen winners of a "first kiss" raffle.

An Invitation

"But when you give a banquet, invite the poor, the crippled, the lame, the blind, and you will be blessed."

— Luke 14:13, 14

Jesus was teaching about the importance of inviting those who could not repay, and then said, "Although they cannot repay you, you will be repaid at the resurrection of the righteous" (Luke 14:14).

Beverly had planned to push the marriage date back to September, but she wasn't happy about it. Now that won't be necessary. Her fiancé, Timothy, came home this week in time for the original June wedding date. The wedding has been scheduled since last August, but they were able to send out the invitations only last week. They sent them to all their friends and family and those they had met during the months of waiting for Timothy's return.

"There are no big immediate plans. The 'welcome home' dinner is lasagna," the bride-in-waiting said.

"We are just thrilled see each other again."

They had a quiet time of enjoying being together, reflecting on the little things: peace, contentment and love.

God's Hand Has Strengthened Us

"So do not fear, for I am with you; do not be dismayed, for I am your God. I will strengthen you and help you; I will uphold you with my righteous right hand."

—Isaiah 41:10

Wayne, a flight engineer, enjoyed a group hug from his wife and daughters. He said he was looking forward to some "good food that has some spices."

"There is nothing like fighting a war together to make everybody realize that we are all professionals," Wayne said.

"It's real moving," he said, "to stand here and watch that plane come in with a U.S. flag hanging out the window. Those are our kids. They're back! And watching all of the family members—the dads, moms, spouses, children—is exciting."

God has been with us, strengthening us, and has brought many back home to their loved ones. Yet, we must remember those who died for our beloved America.

Prayer, Family and Church

"And on this rock I will build my church,,
and the gates of Hades will not overcome it.

—Matthew 16 18

"**E**verything was happening so fast. I didn't get to call everyone and tell them I was leaving," said Joyce, one of the Navy technicians who was assigned to the US Comfort, a Navy ship.

Her notice came only a few days before she had to leave. Joyce insisted she had adjusted well to tight quarters, three-tier bunks, food not always seasoned the way she likes and a minor brush with seasickness.

Joyce called home every two weeks. "I couldn't tell them anything," she said, "except I loved them and I was okay." She sometimes could not sleep. So she read all the books she could find.

"Leaving the kids was the worst part," said Joyce. Mother's Day was especially tough. "I called them."

"Prayer and church are what sustained me. We had an excellent church program onboard. If it hadn't been for that, I probably would have gone crazy a long time ago."

Balloons, Bands and Burgers

Shout for joy to the Lord, all the earth, worship the Lord with gladness; come before him with joyful songs.

—Psalm 100:1-2

Balloons, bands, and burgers were among the featured, or anticipated, attractions early one afternoon as another group returned home after a more-than-four-month deployment in support of Operation Iraqi Freedom.

"The mission was over for those who came back today," said their commander.

June was anxiously awaiting her husband's arrival. "I won't believe it until he gets off the bus," she said. The couple, both from Mississippi, were high school sweethearts and celebrated their twenty-fifth anniversary last November.

"We were a little worried that we would not be able to celebrate before he left," she said, "but we made it." The couple plans a trip to Six Flags in the near future.

Praising God continually and giving thanks are on the hearts of many who are celebrating this wonderful occasion of welcoming their loved ones home.

A Heroes' Welcome

Praise the Lord. Praise God in his sanctuary; praise him in his mighty heavens. Praise him for his acts of power, praise him for his surpassing greatness.

—Psalm 150:1-2

People smiling, children laughing and spouses hugging has been the scene the last few weeks. Although the troops agreed it was nice to be home, they all were proud to have defended our country.

Happy tears streamed down the faces of many who looked on as a young lieutenant held his newborn son in his arms.

Family members were waving flags, holding signs and wearing red, white and blue to show support for their loved ones getting off the plane.

The troops all agreed that it was great to have a heroes' homecoming after an operation that meant so much to the United States.

Home Base Watches as Marines Return

Sons are a heritage from the Lord, children a reward from him. Like arrows in the hands of a warrior are sons born in one's youth. Blessed is the man whose quiver is full of them.

—Psalm 127:3-5

Gloria was barefoot and sodden, her baby clutched in her arms. But her smile brightened the dark, rainy Monday morning as she waited by the ocean for her husband to come home from war.

Families gathered at the base pier at Onslow Beach as their loved ones began riding transport craft to shore from three ships. It was the first major Marine Corps unit to return to the United States.

First to hit the beach were about two dozen Marines driving a small convoy. The group was led off the landing craft by a small bulldozer flying a large American flag.

A number of the returning Marines were getting their first look at sons and daughters born while they were away. The excitement of those Marines, scurrying to hug their wives and children, was a joy to behold.

A Memorial Day Reunion

*Be strong and do not give up, for your
work will be rewarded.*

—2 Chronicles 15:7

Memorial Day was a day of celebration for thousands of soldiers and their families who were reunited after a long deployment. Loved ones gathered together to celebrate this long-awaited homecoming.

President Bush remembered the country's fallen heroes in the traditional Memorial Day wreath-laying ceremony at Arlington National Cemetery's Tomb of the Unknown Soldier. After laying the wreath, Bush paid tribute to those who died at war, noting particularly "recent loss and recent courage" in Iraq and Afghanistan.

"Today we recall that liberty is always the achievement of courage, and today we remember all who have died, all who are still missing and all who mourn," Bush said.

Memories of Those
Who Served

You, my brothers, were called to be free. But do not use your freedom to indulge the sinful nature; rather, serve one another in love.
—*Galatians 5 13*

In New York, the wives of two Marine Corps pilots killed in Iraq dropped a Memorial Day wreath into the Hudson River at the Intrepid Sea-Air-Space Museum's annual ceremony.

A light drizzle didn't stop thousands of people from gathering for a parade along flag-lined Michigan Avenue in Dearborn, Michigan, a Detroit suburb in which about thirty per cent of residents claim Arab ancestry. Yellow ribbons were everywhere—wrapped around trees and traffic signs, on cars and houses.

One Iranian, who came to the United States with his wife eight years ago, said attending the Memorial Day events was a way to say "thank you" to the soldiers who helped liberate his native land.

"We came to share the celebration together with the American people," he said. "This year we are very happy because our old president is gone. We've got freedom in our country."

First Anniversary

I will sing for the one I love a song about his vineyard.

—*Isaiah* : 1

*M*emorial Day marked a first anniversary for one couple. It was the first wedding anniversary and the first time Bill would see the couple's two-month-old daughter.

"As long as he's coming home, that's the best anniversary present you could have," said his wife, who stood patiently by the ocean in the pouring rain. They found out she was pregnant just before the unit departed. "It was hard, but I knew he was coming home and everything would be okay," she said, as she and her family shrugged off the muggy rain.

"I spent a lot of nights thinking about what this day would be like," he said as he looked at his new baby. "I'm just sort of dumbfounded."

A Letter to the Military

Dear American serviceman/woman,

My sons are my world. I want you to know that they are two of the many you are fighting for. They are too young to fully understand, but one day they will know.

I will do my best to make sure they know what you have sacrificed for their futures.

You should know that I am so very grateful for your loyalty, pride and love for America.

I can only pray that my children never have to face such evils as you have to face.

I'm sure your mothers prayed the same. But if my children do have to face evil, I hope they will walk with their shoulders square, their heads held high and their hearts filled with the same determination that you have.

You are all in my thoughts and prayers each day.

I am praying for your safe return and a great victory over our foes.

God bless you all!

—From a mother
Rev Up, the Robins Air Force Base newspaper, May 9, 2003

The Difference

*O*ver the years, I've talked a lot about military spouses—how special they are and the price they pay for freedom, too. The funny thing about it is most military spouses don't consider themselves different from other spouses.

They do what they have to do, bound together not by blood or merely friendship, but with a shared spirit, the origin of which is in the very essence of what love truly is. Is there truly a difference? I think there is. You have to decide for yourself.

Non-military spouses get married and look forward to building equity in a home and putting down family roots. Military spouses get married and know they'll live in base housing or rentals and their roots must be short so they can be transplanted frequently.

Non-military spouses decorate a home with flair and personality that will last a lifetime. Military spouses decorate a home with flair, tempered with the knowledge that no two base houses have the same-sized windows or same-sized rooms. Curtains have to be flexible and multiple sets are a plus. Furniture must fit like puzzle pieces.

Non-military spouses say good-bye to their spouse for a business trip and know they won't see them for a week. They are lonely, but can survive. Military spouses say good-bye to their deploying spouse and know they won't see them for months, or for a remote, a year. They are lonely, but will survive.

Non-military spouses, when a washer hose blows off, call Maytag and then write out a check for getting the hose reconnected. Military spouses will cut the water off and fix it themselves.

Non-military spouses get used to saying "hello" to friends they see all the time. Military spouses get used to saying "good-bye" to friends made the last two years.

Non-military spouses worry about whether their child will be accepted in yet another new school next year.

Non-military spouses can count on spouse participation in special events: birthdays, anniversaries, concerts, football games, graduations, and even the birth of a child. Military spouses only count on each other because they realize that the Flag has to come first if freedom is to survive. It has to be that way.

Non-military spouses put up yellow ribbons when the troops are imperiled across the globe and take them down when the troops come home. Military spouses wear yellow ribbons around their hearts and they never go away.

Non-military spouses worry about being late for Mom's Thanksgiving dinner. Military spouses worry about getting back from Japan in time for Dad's funeral.

And the television program showing an elderly lady putting a card down in front of a long black wall that has names on it touches other spouses. The card simply says, "Happy Birthday, Sweetheart. You would have been sixty today." A military spouse is the one with the card. And the wall is the Vietnam Memorial.

I would never say military spouses are better or worse than other spouses are. But I will say there is a difference.

And I will say that our country asks more of military spouses than is asked of other spouses. And, I will say without hesitation that military spouses pay just as high a price for freedom as do their active-duty husbands or wives.

Perhaps the price they pay is even higher. Dying in service to our country isn't near as hard as loving someone who has died in service to our country and having to live without them.

God bless our military spouses for all they freely give. And God bless America.

—Retired Lt. General Edward J. Heinz
Rev Up, the Robins Air Force Base newspaper, May 16, 2003

About the Author

Judy Davis and her husband Colin live in Warner Robins, Georgia, where they are both employed by the federal government. They have three married children: Bob, Cindi and Tim, and five grandchildren: Ashley, Brandon, Justin, Connor and Noah. Colin and Judy enjoy travelling and seeing the many different lighthouses on the east coast.